breeze-easy method 2

BBᵇ Tuba

by John Kinyon

Cover photo courtesy of the Selmer Company.

FOREWORD

Although this book has been written as a logical sequel to Book I of the Breeze-Easy Method for BBb TUBA, it may be used advantageously as a follow-up to any good beginning method. As in Book I, the Tuba, Trumpet and Trombone books may be used in conjunction with each other, thus facilitating the organization of brass classes.

Four major areas of development are emphasized in each lesson:

1. **EMBOUCHURE DEVELOPMENT** Each lesson has a warm-up exercise, progressing from long tones and easy lip slurs in the early lessons to moderately advanced flexibility studies in the later lessons. Interval studies are also frequently employed to give the student drill in tone placement.

2. **A PLAYING KNOWLEDGE OF SCALES** Each lesson contains concentrated scale practice in the belief that a mastery of scales is essential to general technique and facility.

3. **RHYTHMIC READING** All rhythmic studies are designed to develop independence in reading, and all duets are contrapuntal in style. (In the Tuba book, however, a true bass part has been substituted for the duet part, giving a better sound to mixed brass class ensemble performance.)

4. **DEVELOPING A CONCEPTION OF LEGATO (SONG STYLE) PLAYING** Folk ballads are generously interspersed throughout the book in the belief that the development of a singing tone is a most important, and oft-times most neglected phase of wind instrument performance.

Metronome markings are frequently indicated, serving both as a tempo standard and as a challenge to the student in his daily practice. Each lesson should be thoroughly accomplished before proceeding to the next; there are no short-cuts to musical achievement.

John Kinyon

LESSON 1.

THIS LESSON HAS BEEN COMPLETED. DATE _____ EXCELLENT ☐ GOOD ☐ FAIR ☐

4

LESSON 2.

WARM-UP

2. Play the following scales from memory: B♭, A♭.

LITTLE BROWN JUG

WINNER

PRAIRIE SONG

Traditional

THIS LESSON HAS BEEN COMPLETED.   DATE _____   EXCELLENT ☐   GOOD ☐   FAIR ☐

21642-30

LESSON 3.

KEY OF C	B♮

WARM-UP

Hold each tone 8 slow counts; think of a steady, full tone.
Take the mouthpiece from your lips after each hold.

THE C MAJOR SCALE

2. New Memorize

3. Play slowly, place each tone neatly.

4. 1 + 2 1 da + da 2
New Four sixteenth notes equal one quarter note.

5.

SKIP TO MY LOU

Traditional

6. Melody
staccato
This part for brass class only.

MARCHE SLAVE

TCHAIKOVSKY

7. Maestoso 1. 2.
f

8. Melody
This part for brass class only.

THIS LESSON HAS BEEN COMPLETED. DATE _____ EXCELLENT ☐ GOOD ☐ FAIR ☐

LESSON 4.

DOTTED EIGHTH AND SIXTEENTH NOTES

WARM-UP

1. Take big breaths and play slowly.

2. Play the following scales from memory: Bb, Ab, C.

3. These measures are played the same.

4.

HERE COMES THE BRIDE
WAGNER

5. Maestoso

6. (A) (B) (C)   Traditional Round

7. Play these exercises lightly and neatly.
Your goal in a week's time should be (♩=72).*

ENGLISH BALLAD
Traditional

8. Andante

*This is called a metronome marking and indicates the number of beats per minute.

THIS LESSON HAS BEEN COMPLETED. DATE _____ EXCELLENT ☐ GOOD ☐ FAIR ☐

LESSON 5.

| **Allegretto** = *Quickly (but not as fast as Allegro)* |
| **Moderato** = *At a medium tempo* |

WARM-UP

Play these exercises very slowly.
Try to produce a big, full tone.

1.

2. Play the following scales from memory. Bb, Ab, C.

OLD KING COLE

New **Allegretto**   Traditional

3.   *mf*

OH, MY DARLING CLEMENTINE

New **Moderato**   Traditional

4.

REVIEW ETUDE

(♩ = 112)

5.   *mf*

G# = Ab   F# = Gb

THIS LESSON HAS BEEN COMPLETED. DATE _____ EXCELLENT ☐ GOOD ☐ FAIR ☐

LESSON 6.

REVIEW LESSON

WARM-UP

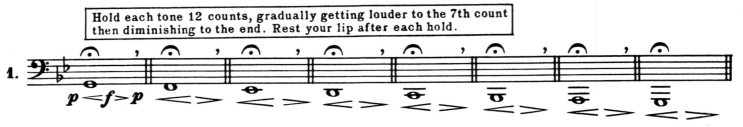

Hold each tone 12 counts, gradually getting louder to the 7th count then diminishing to the end. Rest your lip after each hold.

2. Play the following scales from memory: Bb, Ab, C.

Place each tone neatly and accurately.

Moderato

Allegretto

OH! SUSANNA

FOSTER

REVIEW ETUDE

(♩ = 100)

THIS LESSON HAS BEEN COMPLETED. DATE _____ EXCELLENT ☐ GOOD ☐ FAIR ☐

LESSON 7.

KEY OF Db **HIGH Db** $\frac{3}{8}$ $\frac{6}{8}$

WARM-UP

Play slowly and smoothly.

THE Db MAJOR SCALE

New **Memorize**

Play slowly and place every tone neatly. Listen to each pitch.

DRINK TO ME ONLY WITH THINE EYES

Moderato

Traditional

21642-30

LESSON 8.

ENHARMONICS (𝄾 in 3/8 and 6/8)

WARM-UP

Play these exercises slowly, trying for a full, even tone.

1.

2. Play the following scales from memory: B♭, A♭, C, D♭.

OLD FRIENDS WITH NEW NAMES*

3.

4.

5.

WHEN LOVE IS KIND

Traditional

Moderato

6.

*Notes connected by arrows indicate enharmonic tones. These are tones which sound alike although written differently. The fingerings are the same. For further explanation refer to chart on top of page 32.

THIS LESSON HAS BEEN COMPLETED. DATE _____ EXCELLENT ☐ GOOD ☐ FAIR ☐

LESSON 9.

CHROMATIC SCALE (♪♩ in 3/8 and 6/8)

WARM-UP

Play slowly with a big, open tone.

1.

A CHROMATIC SCALE

2. **Memorize**

AN ENHARMONIC TEASER

3. **Name this tune**

4.

SCOTCH BALLAD

Andante

SPILMAN

5.

THIS LESSON HAS BEEN COMPLETED. DATE _____ EXCELLENT ☐ GOOD ☐ FAIR ☐

LESSON 10.

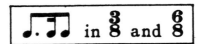 in $\frac{3}{8}$ and $\frac{6}{8}$

WARM-UP

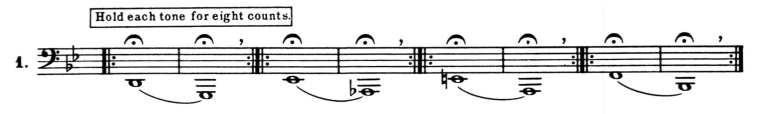

2. Play the following scales from memory: B♭, A♭, C, D♭ Chromatic.

BONNY DOON

Moderato

Traditional

Allegretto

THIS LESSON HAS BEEN COMPLETED. DATE _____ EXCELLENT☐ GOOD☐ FAIR☐

LESSON 11.

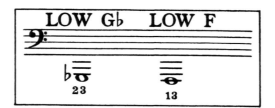

LOW Gb   LOW F

WARM-UP

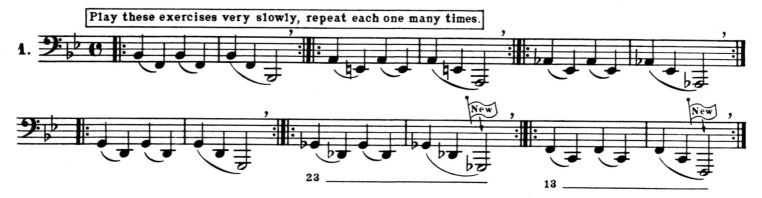

2 Play the following scales from memory: Bb, Ab, C, Db, Chromatic.

HOME ON THE RANGE

Traditional

THIS LESSON HAS BEEN COMPLETED.   DATE _____ EXCELLENT ☐   GOOD ☐   FAIR ☐

21642-30

LESSON 12.

REVIEW LESSON

WARM-UP

Repeat each exercise many times. Rest your lip frequently.

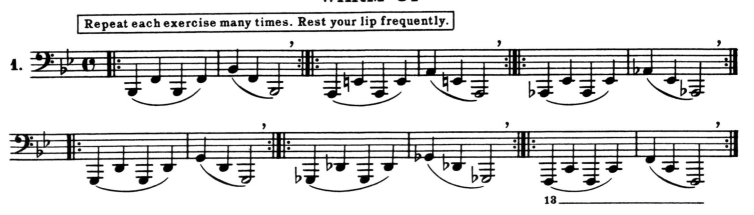

2. Play the following scales from memory: Bb, Ab, C, Db, Chromatic.

REVIEW ETUDE

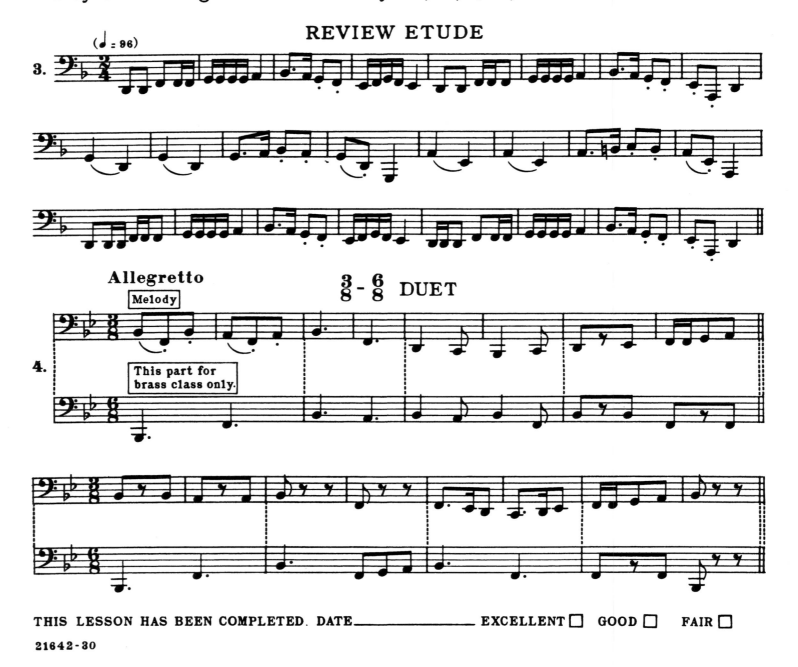

Allegretto

Melody

$\frac{3}{8}$ - $\frac{6}{8}$ DUET

This part for brass class only.

4.

THIS LESSON HAS BEEN COMPLETED. DATE_____ EXCELLENT ☐ GOOD ☐ FAIR ☐

*The second player plays two measures behind the first.
THIS LESSON HAS BEEN COMPLETED. DATE_____ EXCELLENT ☐ GOOD ☐ FAIR ☐

LESSON 14.

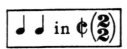

WARM-UP

> Play these exercises slowly. Think a big sound.
> Nothing is more important than a good tone.

2. Play the following scales from memory: Bb, Ab, C, Db, Eb, Chromatic.

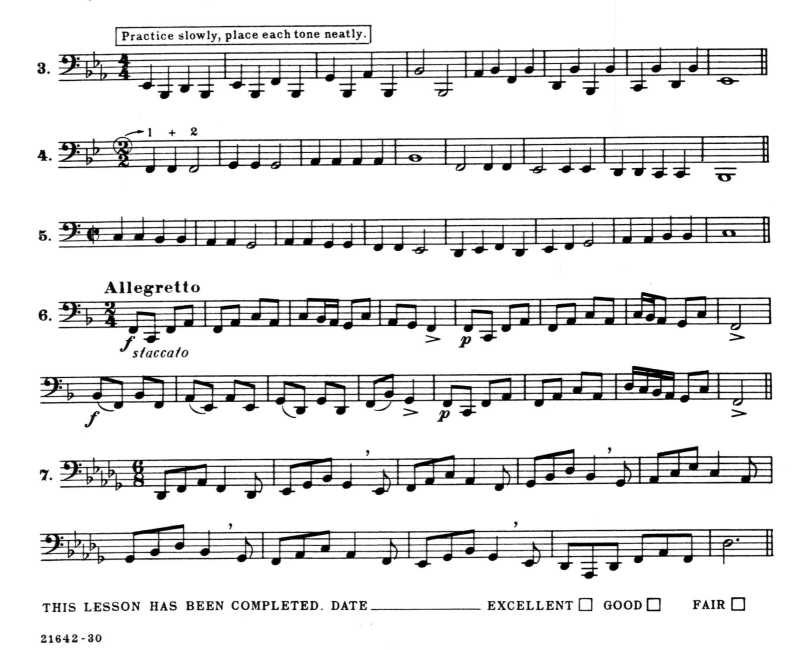

> Practice slowly, place each tone neatly.

THIS LESSON HAS BEEN COMPLETED. DATE _____ EXCELLENT ☐ GOOD ☐ FAIR ☐

LESSON 15.

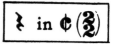

WARM-UP

Take big breaths and blow in an open, relaxed manner. Rest your lip frequently.

2. Play the following scales from memory: Bb, Ab, C, Db, Eb, Chromatic.

Allegretto

SOLO ETUDE

J. K.

THIS LESSON HAS BEEN COMPLETED. DATE _____ EXCELLENT ☐ GOOD ☐ FAIR ☐

LESSON 16.

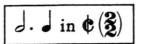

WARM-UP

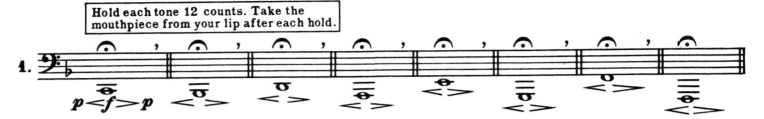

Hold each tone 12 counts. Take the mouthpiece from your lip after each hold.

1.

2. Play the following scales from memory: Bb, Ab, C, Db, Eb, Chromatic.

THIS LESSON HAS BEEN COMPLETED. DATE_____ EXCELLENT ☐ GOOD ☐ FAIR ☐

LESSON 17.

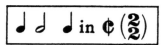

WARM-UP

Play slowly. Rest your lip frequently.

2. Play the following scales from memory: Bb, Ab, C, Db, Eb, Chromatic.

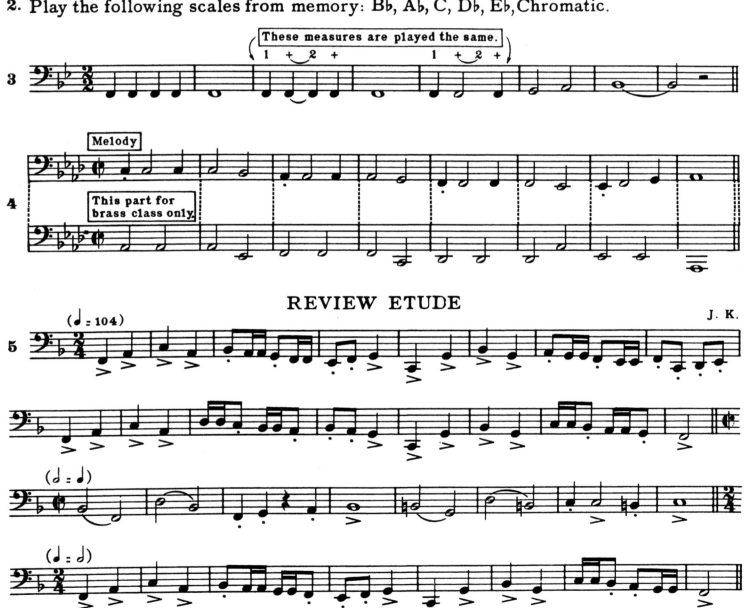

REVIEW ETUDE

J. K.

THIS LESSON HAS BEEN COMPLETED. DATE_____ EXCELLENT ☐ GOOD ☐ FAIR ☐

LESSON 18.

REVIEW LESSON

WARM-UP

Take big breaths. Rest your lip frequently.

2. Play the following scales from memory: B♭, A♭, C, D♭, E♭, Chromatic.

REVIEW ETUDE

J. K.

THE YELLOW ROSE OF TEXAS

Allegretto   Traditional

THIS LESSON HAS BEEN COMPLETED. DATE _____ EXCELLENT ☐   GOOD ☐   FAIR ☐

LESSON 19.

HIGH E   HIGH F

$\frac{6}{8}$ in **2** ($\left(\downarrow. \quad \downarrow. \text{ in } \frac{6}{8} \text{ (in 2)}\right)$

WARM-UP
Hold each tone 12 counts. Rest your lip after each hold.

THE F MAJOR SCALE
Memorize

Place each tone neatly.

*New Count → 1 2 1 2 1 2 1 2

(in 2) Melody

This part for brass class only. (in 2)

IRISH BALLAD
Moderato

*At fast tempos it is more convenient to count only two beats in each $\frac{6}{8}$ measure.

THIS LESSON HAS BEEN COMPLETED. DATE_____ EXCELLENT ☐ GOOD ☐ FAIR ☐

21642-30

LESSON 20.

WARM-UP

Play these exercises very slowly. Practice only the keys you can play without forcing the tone.

2. Play the following scales from memory: Bb, Ab, C, Db, Eb, F, Chromatic.

ALL THROUGH THE NIGHT

Traditional

* Three equal notes to the beat are called a triplet.

THIS LESSON HAS BEEN COMPLETED. DATE _____ EXCELLENT ☐ GOOD ☐ FAIR ☐

LESSON 21.

$$\frac{9}{8} \left(\text{♩ ♪ in } \frac{6}{8} \text{ (in 2) and } \frac{9}{8} \text{ (in 3)} \right)$$

WARM-UP

Hold each tone 12 slow counts. Keep the air pressure steady and try to focus your tone.

2. Play the following scales from memory: B♭, A♭, C, D♭, E♭, F, Chromatic.

(in 2)

These measures are played the same.

Allegretto
(in 2)

Allegretto
(in 2)

THREE BLIND MICE

Traditional Round

Moderato
(in 3)

BEAUTIFUL DREAMER

FOSTER

(in 9)

ritard.

THIS LESSON HAS BEEN COMPLETED. DATE _____ EXCELLENT ☐ GOOD ☐ FAIR ☐

LESSON 22.

WARM-UP

THIS LESSON HAS BEEN COMPLETED. DATE _____ EXCELLENT ☐ GOOD ☐ FAIR ☐

LESSON 23.

REVIEW LESSON

WARM-UP

Take big breaths. Do not force the tone.

2. Play the following scales in eighth notes:
Bb, Ab, C, Db, Eb, F, G, Chromatic.

KEY AND RHYTHMIC REVIEW

J. K.

(in 2) **Melody**

(in 2) This part for brass class only.

Moderato
(in 3)

THE ASH GROVE

Traditional
Fine

D. C. al Fine

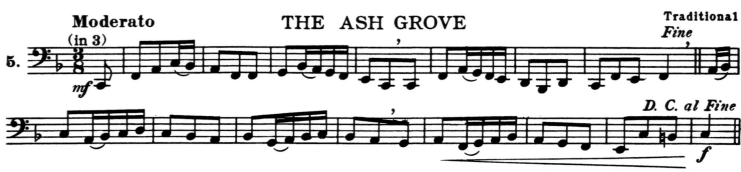

THIS LESSON HAS BEEN COMPLETED. DATE ———————— EXCELLENT ☐ GOOD ☐ FAIR ☐

21642-30

LESSON 24.

REVIEW LESSON

WARM-UP

> Play these exercises slowly. Try to carry the full, open sound of the low register into the high register.

2. Play the following scales in eighth notes: Bb, Ab, C, Db, Eb, F, G, Chromatic. (♩ = 104)

> Place each tone neatly.

3.

6/8 REVIEW ETUDE

Allegretto (in 2)   J. K.

4.

JEANIE WITH THE LIGHT BROWN HAIR

Andante   FOSTER

5.

THIS LESSON HAS BEEN COMPLETED. DATE _____ EXCELLENT ☐   GOOD ☐   FAIR ☐

LESSON 25.

REVIEW LESSON

WARM-UP

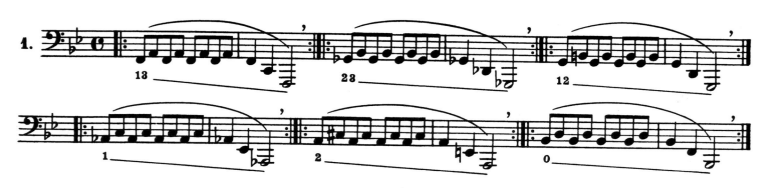

2. Play the following scales in eighth notes: Bb, Ab, C, Db, Eb, F, G, Chromatic.

THIS LESSON HAS BEEN COMPLETED. DATE _____ EXCELLENT ☐ GOOD ☐ FAIR ☐

21642-30

LESSON 26.

REVIEW LESSON

WARM-UP

2. Play the following scales in eighth notes: ($\flat$ = 120) B$\flat$, A$\flat$, C, D$\flat$, E$\flat$, F, G, Chromatic.

REVIEW ETUDE

J. K.

THIS LESSON HAS BEEN COMPLETED. DATE _____ EXCELLENT ☐   GOOD ☐   FAIR ☐

LESSON 27.

REVIEW LESSON

WARM-UP

2. Play the following scales in eighth notes: B♭, A♭, C, D♭, E♭, F, G, Chromatic.

Play this exercise slowly. Listen carefully to each pitch.

REVIEW ETUDE

THIS LESSON HAS BEEN COMPLETED. DATE_____ EXCELLENT ☐ GOOD ☐ FAIR ☐

21642-30

LESSON 28.

REVIEW LESSON

WARM-UP

2. Play the following scales in eighth notes: (♩=132) Bb, Ab, C, Db, Eb, F, G, Chromatic.

NOBODY KNOWS THE TROUBLE I'VE SEEN

Traditional Spiritual

REVIEW ETUDE

J. K.

THIS LESSON HAS BEEN COMPLETED. DATE _____ EXCELLENT ☐ GOOD ☐ FAIR ☐

MAJOR* SCALES LEARNED IN THIS BOOK

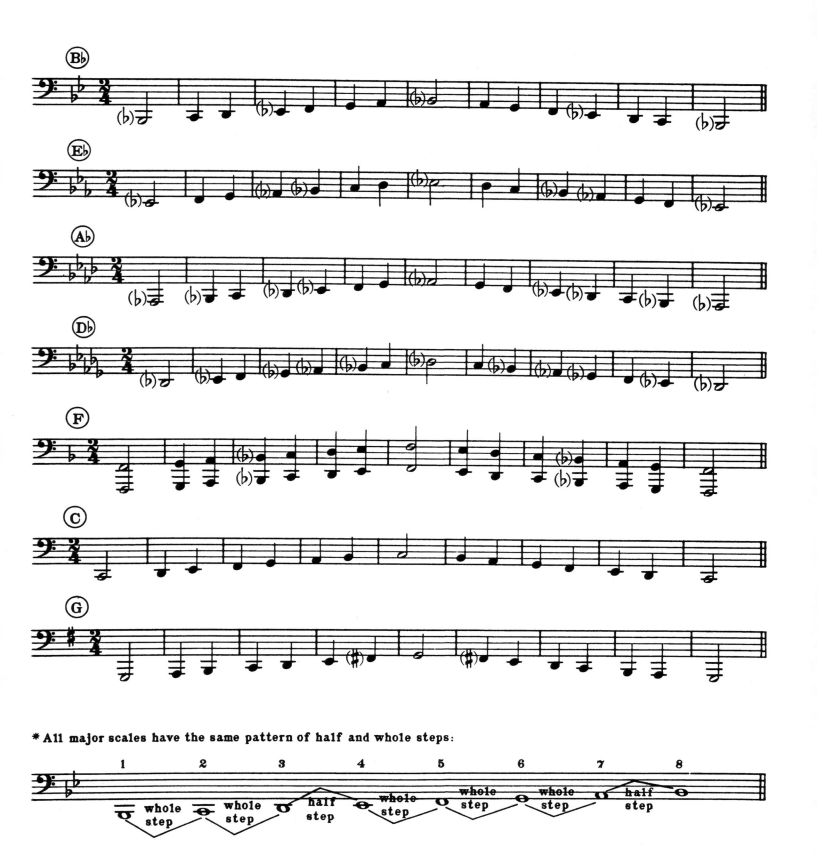

*All major scales have the same pattern of half and whole steps:

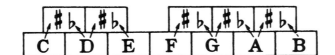

CHART OF FINGERINGS

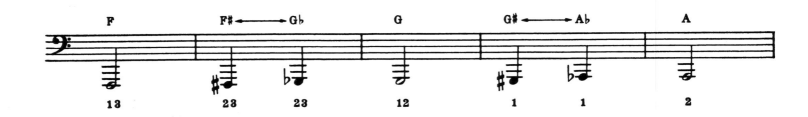

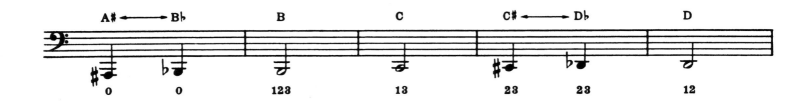

21642-30